THIS BOOK BELONGS TO:

Vital Info

Name :

Date of Birth :

SSN :

Weight :

Blood Type :

Primary Dr. :

Dr. Phone :

Dr. Address :

Dentist Name :

Dentist Phone :

Dentist Address :

NOTE :

Milestone Tracker

DATE	
. .	
. .	
. .	
. .	
. .	
. .	
. .	
. .	
. .	
. .	
. .	
. .	
. .	
. .	
. .	
. .	
. .	
. .	
. .	
. .	
. .	
. .	
. .	

Milestone Tracker

DATE	
· ·	
· ·	
· ·	
· ·	
· ·	
· ·	
· ·	
· ·	
· ·	
· ·	
· ·	
· ·	
· ·	
· ·	
· ·	
· ·	
· ·	
· ·	
· ·	
· ·	
· ·	
· ·	
· ·	

Week 01 | Child Goals

Date : _____/_____/_____

SPEECH & COMMUNICATION

_____ ☐
_____ ☐
_____ ☐
_____ ☐
_____ ☐
_____ ☐

SOCIAL SKILLS

_____ ☐
_____ ☐
_____ ☐
_____ ☐
_____ ☐
_____ ☐

SENSORY

_____ ☐
_____ ☐
_____ ☐
_____ ☐
_____ ☐
_____ ☐

Week 01 | Activities Days & Activity Ideas

MONDAY

TUESDAY

WEDNESDAY

THURSDAY

FRIDAY

SATURDAY

SUNDAY

FINE MOTOR ACTIVITIES

VESTIBULAR-PROPRIOCEPTIVE

TACTILE

VISUAL

ORAL

AUDITORY

NOTE

Week **01** | Goals & Progress
Tracker

Date : _____/_____/_____

SPEECH & COMMUNICATION :

SOCIAL SKILLS :

SENSORY :

VESTIBULAR :

VISUAL :

TACTILE :

ORAL MOTOR :

AUDITORY :

FINE MOTOR :

THIS WEEK'S CHALLENGES :

THIS WEEK'S HIGHLIGHTS :

FAVORITE MOMENT :

Week 01 | Appointment

MON: ☐

TUE: ☐

WED: ☐

THU: ☐

FRI: ☐

SAT: ☐

SUN: ☐

Week 02 | Child Goals

Date : _____/_____/_____

SPEECH & COMMUNICATION

_____ ☐
_____ ☐
_____ ☐
_____ ☐
_____ ☐
_____ ☐

SOCIAL SKILLS

_____ ☐
_____ ☐
_____ ☐
_____ ☐
_____ ☐
_____ ☐

SENSORY

_____ ☐
_____ ☐
_____ ☐
_____ ☐
_____ ☐
_____ ☐

Week 02 | Activities Days & Activity Ideas

MONDAY

TUESDAY

WEDNESDAY

THURSDAY

FRIDAY

SATURDAY

SUNDAY

FINE MOTOR ACTIVITIES

VESTIBULAR-PROPRIOCEPTIVE

TACTILE

VISUAL

ORAL

AUDITORY

NOTE

Week 02

Goals & Progress
Tracker

Date : _____/_____/_____

SPEECH & COMMUNICATION :

SOCIAL SKILLS :

SENSORY :

VESTIBULAR :

VISUAL :

TACTILE :

ORAL MOTOR :

AUDITORY :

FINE MOTOR :

THIS WEEK'S CHALLENGES :

THIS WEEK'S HIGHLIGHTS :

FAVORITE MOMENT :

Week 02 | Appointment

MON: ☐

TUE: ☐

WED: ☐

THU: ☐

FRI: ☐

SAT: ☐

SUN: ☐

Week 03 | Child Goals

Date : _____/_____/_____

SPEECH & COMMUNICATION

_____ ☐
_____ ☐
_____ ☐
_____ ☐
_____ ☐
_____ ☐

SOCIAL SKILLS

_____ ☐
_____ ☐
_____ ☐
_____ ☐
_____ ☐
_____ ☐

SENSORY

_____ ☐
_____ ☐
_____ ☐
_____ ☐
_____ ☐
_____ ☐

Week 03 | Activities Days & Activity Ideas

MONDAY

TUESDAY

WEDNESDAY

THURSDAY

FRIDAY

SATURDAY

SUNDAY

FINE MOTOR ACTIVITIES

VESTIBULAR-PROPRIOCEPTIVE

TACTILE

VISUAL

ORAL

AUDITORY

NOTE

Week 03 | Goals & Progress
Tracker

Date : _____/_____/_____

SPEECH & COMMUNICATION :

SOCIAL SKILLS :

SENSORY :

VESTIBULAR :

VISUAL :

TACTILE :

ORAL MOTOR :

AUDITORY :

FINE MOTOR :

THIS WEEK'S CHALLENGES :

THIS WEEK'S HIGHLIGHTS :

FAVORITE MOMENT :

Week **03** | **Appointment**

MON: ☐

TUE: ☐

WED: ☐

THU: ☐

FRI: ☐

SAT: ☐

SUN: ☐

Week 04 | Child Goals

Date : _____/_____/_____

SPEECH & COMMUNICATION

_____ ☐
_____ ☐
_____ ☐
_____ ☐
_____ ☐
_____ ☐

SOCIAL SKILLS

_____ ☐
_____ ☐
_____ ☐
_____ ☐
_____ ☐
_____ ☐

SENSORY

_____ ☐
_____ ☐
_____ ☐
_____ ☐
_____ ☐
_____ ☐

Week 04 | Activities Days & Activity Ideas

MONDAY

TUESDAY

WEDNESDAY

THURSDAY

FRIDAY

SATURDAY

SUNDAY

FINE MOTOR ACTIVITIES

VESTIBULAR-PROPRIOCEPTIVE

TACTILE

VISUAL

ORAL

AUDITORY

NOTE

Week **04** | Goals & Progress
Tracker Date : ____ / ____ / _____

SPEECH & COMMUNICATION :

SOCIAL SKILLS :

SENSORY :

VESTIBULAR :

VISUAL :

TACTILE :

ORAL MOTOR :

AUDITORY :

FINE MOTOR :

THIS WEEK'S CHALLENGES :

THIS WEEK'S HIGHLIGHTS :

FAVORITE MOMENT :

Week **04** | **Appointment**

☐

MON:

☐

TUE:

☐

WED:

☐

THU:

☐

FRI:

☐

SAT:

☐

SUN:

Week 05 | Child Goals

Date : _____/_____/_____

SPEECH & COMMUNICATION

☐
☐
☐
☐
☐
☐

SOCIAL SKILLS

☐
☐
☐
☐
☐
☐

SENSORY

☐
☐
☐
☐
☐
☐

Week 05 | Activities Days & Activity Ideas

MONDAY

TUESDAY

WEDNESDAY

THURSDAY

FRIDAY

SATURDAY

SUNDAY

FINE MOTOR ACTIVITIES

VESTIBULAR-PROPRIOCEPTIVE

TACTILE

VISUAL

ORAL

AUDITORY

NOTE

Week 05 | Goals & Progress
Tracker

Date : _____ / _____ / _____

SPEECH & COMMUNICATION :

SOCIAL SKILLS :

SENSORY :

VESTIBULAR :

VISUAL :

TACTILE :

ORAL MOTOR :

AUDITORY :

FINE MOTOR :

THIS WEEK'S CHALLENGES :

THIS WEEK'S HIGHLIGHTS :

FAVORITE MOMENT :

Week 05 | Appointment

MON: ☐

TUE: ☐

WED: ☐

THU: ☐

FRI: ☐

SAT: ☐

SUN: ☐

NOTE

Week 06 | Child Goals

Date : _____/_____/_____

SPEECH & COMMUNICATION

_____ ☐
_____ ☐
_____ ☐
_____ ☐
_____ ☐
_____ ☐

SOCIAL SKILLS

_____ ☐
_____ ☐
_____ ☐
_____ ☐
_____ ☐
_____ ☐

SENSORY

_____ ☐
_____ ☐
_____ ☐
_____ ☐
_____ ☐
_____ ☐

Week 06 | Activities Days & Activity Ideas

MONDAY

TUESDAY

WEDNESDAY

THURSDAY

FRIDAY

SATURDAY

SUNDAY

FINE MOTOR ACTIVITIES

VESTIBULAR-PROPRIOCEPTIVE

TACTILE

VISUAL

ORAL

AUDITORY

NOTE

Week 06 | Goals & Progress
Tracker

Date : _____ / _____ / _____

SPEECH & COMMUNICATION :

SOCIAL SKILLS :

SENSORY :

VESTIBULAR :

VISUAL :

TACTILE :

ORAL MOTOR :

AUDITORY :

FINE MOTOR :

THIS WEEK'S CHALLENGES :

THIS WEEK'S HIGHLIGHTS :

FAVORITE MOMENT :

Week 06 | Appointment

MON: ☐

TUE: ☐

WED: ☐

THU: ☐

FRI: ☐

SAT: ☐

SUN: ☐

Week 07 | Child Goals

Date : _____/_____/_____

SPEECH & COMMUNICATION

☐

☐

☐

☐

☐

☐

SOCIAL SKILLS

☐

☐

☐

☐

☐

☐

SENSORY

☐

☐

☐

☐

☐

☐

Week 07 | Activities Days & Activity Ideas

MONDAY

TUESDAY

WEDNESDAY

THURSDAY

FRIDAY

SATURDAY

SUNDAY

FINE MOTOR ACTIVITIES

VESTIBULAR-PROPRIOCEPTIVE

TACTILE

VISUAL

ORAL

AUDITORY

NOTE

Week 07 | Goals & Progress
Tracker

Date : _____/_____/_____

SPEECH & COMMUNICATION :

SOCIAL SKILLS :

SENSORY :

VESTIBULAR :

VISUAL :

TACTILE :

ORAL MOTOR :

AUDITORY :

FINE MOTOR :

THIS WEEK'S CHALLENGES :

THIS WEEK'S HIGHLIGHTS :

FAVORITE MOMENT :

Week **07** | **Appointment**

MON: ☐

TUE: ☐

WED: ☐

THU: ☐

FRI: ☐

SAT: ☐

SUN: ☐

Week 08 | Child Goals

SPEECH & COMMUNICATION

_____ ☐

_____ ☐

_____ ☐

_____ ☐

_____ ☐

_____ ☐

SOCIAL SKILLS

_____ ☐

_____ ☐

_____ ☐

_____ ☐

_____ ☐

_____ ☐

SENSORY

_____ ☐

_____ ☐

_____ ☐

_____ ☐

_____ ☐

_____ ☐

Week 08 | Activities Days & Activity Ideas

MONDAY

TUESDAY

WEDNESDAY

THURSDAY

FRIDAY

SATURDAY

SUNDAY

FINE MOTOR ACTIVITIES

VESTIBULAR-PROPRIOCEPTIVE

TACTILE

VISUAL

ORAL

AUDITORY

NOTE

Week 08 | Goals & Progress
Tracker

Date : _____/_____/_____

SPEECH & COMMUNICATION :

SOCIAL SKILLS :

SENSORY :

VESTIBULAR :

VISUAL :

TACTILE :

ORAL MOTOR :

AUDITORY :

FINE MOTOR :

THIS WEEK'S CHALLENGES :

THIS WEEK'S HIGHLIGHTS :

FAVORITE MOMENT :

Week 08 | Appointment

MON: ☐

TUE: ☐

WED: ☐

THU: ☐

FRI: ☐

SAT: ☐

SUN: ☐

Week 09 | Child Goals

Date : _____ / _____ / _____

SPEECH & COMMUNICATION

_____ ☐

_____ ☐

_____ ☐

_____ ☐

_____ ☐

_____ ☐

SOCIAL SKILLS

_____ ☐

_____ ☐

_____ ☐

_____ ☐

_____ ☐

_____ ☐

SENSORY

_____ ☐

_____ ☐

_____ ☐

_____ ☐

_____ ☐

_____ ☐

Week 09 | Activities Days & Activity Ideas

MONDAY

TUESDAY

WEDNESDAY

THURSDAY

FRIDAY

SATURDAY

SUNDAY

FINE MOTOR ACTIVITIES

VESTIBULAR-PROPRIOCEPTIVE

TACTILE

VISUAL

ORAL

AUDITORY

NOTE

Week 09 | Goals & Progress
Tracker

Date : _____/_____/_____

SPEECH & COMMUNICATION :

SOCIAL SKILLS :

SENSORY :

VESTIBULAR :

VISUAL :

TACTILE :

ORAL MOTOR :

AUDITORY :

FINE MOTOR :

THIS WEEK'S CHALLENGES :

THIS WEEK'S HIGHLIGHTS :

FAVORITE MOMENT :

Week **09** | **Appointment**

MON: ☐

TUE: ☐

WED: ☐

THU: ☐

FRI: ☐

SAT: ☐

SUN: ☐

Week 10 | Child Goals

Date : _____/_____/_____

SPEECH & COMMUNICATION

☐
☐
☐
☐
☐
☐

SOCIAL SKILLS

☐
☐
☐
☐
☐
☐

SENSORY

☐
☐
☐
☐
☐
☐

Week 10 | Activities Days & Activity Ideas

MONDAY

TUESDAY

WEDNESDAY

THURSDAY

FRIDAY

SATURDAY

SUNDAY

FINE MOTOR ACTIVITIES

VESTIBULAR-PROPRIOCEPTIVE

TACTILE

VISUAL

ORAL

AUDITORY

NOTE

Week 10 | Goals & Progress
Tracker

Date : _____/_____/_____

SPEECH & COMMUNICATION :

SOCIAL SKILLS :

SENSORY :

VESTIBULAR :

VISUAL :

TACTILE :

ORAL MOTOR :

AUDITORY :

FINE MOTOR :

THIS WEEK'S CHALLENGES :

THIS WEEK'S HIGHLIGHTS :

FAVORITE MOMENT :

Week **10** | **Appointment**

MON: ☐

TUE: ☐

WED: ☐

THU: ☐

FRI: ☐

SAT: ☐

SUN: ☐

Week 11 | Child Goals

Date : _____/_____/_____

SPEECH & COMMUNICATION

☐
☐
☐
☐
☐
☐

SOCIAL SKILLS

☐
☐
☐
☐
☐
☐

SENSORY

☐
☐
☐
☐
☐
☐

Week 11 | Activities Days & Activity Ideas

MONDAY

TUESDAY

WEDNESDAY

THURSDAY

FRIDAY

SATURDAY

SUNDAY

FINE MOTOR ACTIVITIES

VESTIBULAR-PROPRIOCEPTIVE

TACTILE

VISUAL

ORAL

AUDITORY

NOTE

Week 11 | Goals & Progress
Tracker

Date : _____/_____/_____

SPEECH & COMMUNICATION :

SOCIAL SKILLS :

SENSORY :

VESTIBULAR :

VISUAL :

TACTILE :

ORAL MOTOR :

AUDITORY :

FINE MOTOR :

THIS WEEK'S CHALLENGES :

THIS WEEK'S HIGHLIGHTS :

FAVORITE MOMENT :

Week **11** | **Appointment**

MON: ☐

TUE: ☐

WED: ☐

THU: ☐

FRI: ☐

SAT: ☐

SUN: ☐

Week 12 | Child Goals

Date : _____/_____/_____

SPEECH & COMMUNICATION

- ☐
- ☐
- ☐
- ☐
- ☐
- ☐

SOCIAL SKILLS

- ☐
- ☐
- ☐
- ☐
- ☐
- ☐

SENSORY

- ☐
- ☐
- ☐
- ☐
- ☐
- ☐

Week 12 | Activities Days & Activity Ideas

MONDAY

TUESDAY

WEDNESDAY

THURSDAY

FRIDAY

SATURDAY

SUNDAY

FINE MOTOR ACTIVITIES

VESTIBULAR-PROPRIOCEPTIVE

TACTILE

VISUAL

ORAL

AUDITORY

NOTE

Week **12** | Goals & Progress **Tracker** Date : ____ / ____ / _____

SPEECH & COMMUNICATION :

SOCIAL SKILLS :

SENSORY :

VESTIBULAR :

VISUAL :

TACTILE :

ORAL MOTOR :

AUDITORY :

FINE MOTOR :

THIS WEEK'S CHALLENGES :

THIS WEEK'S HIGHLIGHTS :

FAVORITE MOMENT :

Week **12** | **Appointment**

MON: ☐

TUE: ☐

WED: ☐

THU: ☐

FRI: ☐

SAT: ☐

SUN: ☐

Week 13 | Child Goals

Date : _____/_____/_____

SPEECH & COMMUNICATION

_____ ☐

_____ ☐

_____ ☐

_____ ☐

_____ ☐

_____ ☐

SOCIAL SKILLS

_____ ☐

_____ ☐

_____ ☐

_____ ☐

_____ ☐

_____ ☐

SENSORY

_____ ☐

_____ ☐

_____ ☐

_____ ☐

_____ ☐

_____ ☐

Week 13 | Activities Days & Activity Ideas

MONDAY

TUESDAY

WEDNESDAY

THURSDAY

FRIDAY

SATURDAY

SUNDAY

FINE MOTOR ACTIVITIES

VESTIBULAR-PROPRIOCEPTIVE

TACTILE

VISUAL

ORAL

AUDITORY

NOTE

Week 13 | Goals & Progress Tracker

Date : _____/_____/_____

SPEECH & COMMUNICATION :

SOCIAL SKILLS :

SENSORY :

VESTIBULAR :

VISUAL :

TACTILE :

ORAL MOTOR :

AUDITORY :

FINE MOTOR :

THIS WEEK'S CHALLENGES :

THIS WEEK'S HIGHLIGHTS :

FAVORITE MOMENT :

Week **13** | **Appointment**

MON: ☐

TUE: ☐

WED: ☐

THU: ☐

FRI: ☐

SAT: ☐

SUN: ☐

Week 14 | Child Goals

Date : _____/_____/_____

SPEECH & COMMUNICATION

☐

☐

☐

☐

☐

☐

SOCIAL SKILLS

☐

☐

☐

☐

☐

☐

SENSORY

☐

☐

☐

☐

☐

☐

Week 14 | Activities Days & Activity Ideas

MONDAY

TUESDAY

WEDNESDAY

THURSDAY

FRIDAY

SATURDAY

SUNDAY

FINE MOTOR ACTIVITIES

VESTIBULAR-PROPRIOCEPTIVE

TACTILE

VISUAL

ORAL

AUDITORY

NOTE

Week **14** | Goals & Progress **Tracker**

Date : _____ / _____ / _____

SPEECH & COMMUNICATION :

SOCIAL SKILLS :

SENSORY :

VESTIBULAR :

VISUAL :

TACTILE :

ORAL MOTOR :

AUDITORY :

FINE MOTOR :

THIS WEEK'S CHALLENGES :

THIS WEEK'S HIGHLIGHTS :

FAVORITE MOMENT :

Week **14** | **Appointment**

☐

MON:

☐

TUE:

☐

WED:

☐

THU:

☐

FRI:

☐

SAT:

☐

SUN:

Week 15 | Child Goals

Date : _____/_____/_____

SPEECH & COMMUNICATION

☐
☐
☐
☐
☐
☐

SOCIAL SKILLS

☐
☐
☐
☐
☐
☐

SENSORY

☐
☐
☐
☐
☐
☐

Week 15 | Activities Days & Activity Ideas

MONDAY

TUESDAY

WEDNESDAY

THURSDAY

FRIDAY

SATURDAY

SUNDAY

FINE MOTOR ACTIVITIES

VESTIBULAR-PROPRIOCEPTIVE

TACTILE

VISUAL

ORAL

AUDITORY

NOTE

Week 15 | Goals & Progress
Tracker
Date : _____/_____/_____

SPEECH & COMMUNICATION :

SOCIAL SKILLS :

SENSORY :

VESTIBULAR :

VISUAL :

TACTILE :

ORAL MOTOR :

AUDITORY :

FINE MOTOR :

THIS WEEK'S CHALLENGES :

THIS WEEK'S HIGHLIGHTS :

FAVORITE MOMENT :

Week **15** | **Appointment**

MON: ☐

TUE: ☐

WED: ☐

THU: ☐

FRI: ☐

SAT: ☐

SUN: ☐

NOTE

Week 16 | Child Goals

Date : _____/_____/_____

SPEECH & COMMUNICATION

- ☐
- ☐
- ☐
- ☐
- ☐
- ☐

SOCIAL SKILLS

- ☐
- ☐
- ☐
- ☐
- ☐
- ☐

SENSORY

- ☐
- ☐
- ☐
- ☐
- ☐
- ☐

Week 16 | Activities Days & Activity Ideas

MONDAY

TUESDAY

WEDNESDAY

THURSDAY

FRIDAY

SATURDAY

SUNDAY

FINE MOTOR ACTIVITIES

VESTIBULAR-PROPRIOCEPTIVE

TACTILE

VISUAL

ORAL

AUDITORY

NOTE

Week **16** | Goals & Progress
Tracker Date : _____/_____/_____

SPEECH & COMMUNICATION :

SOCIAL SKILLS :

SENSORY :

VESTIBULAR :

VISUAL :

TACTILE :

ORAL MOTOR :

AUDITORY :

FINE MOTOR :

THIS WEEK'S CHALLENGES :

THIS WEEK'S HIGHLIGHTS :

FAVORITE MOMENT :

Week **16** | **Appointment**

MON: ☐

TUE: ☐

WED: ☐

THU: ☐

FRI: ☐

SAT: ☐

SUN: ☐

NOTE

Week 17 | Child Goals

Date : _____/_____/_____

SPEECH & COMMUNICATION

☐
☐
☐
☐
☐
☐

SOCIAL SKILLS

☐
☐
☐
☐
☐
☐

SENSORY

☐
☐
☐
☐
☐
☐

Week 17 | Activities Days & Activity Ideas

MONDAY

TUESDAY

WEDNESDAY

THURSDAY

FRIDAY

SATURDAY

SUNDAY

FINE MOTOR ACTIVITIES

VESTIBULAR-PROPRIOCEPTIVE

TACTILE

VISUAL

ORAL

AUDITORY

NOTE

Week **17** | Goals & Progress
Tracker
Date : _____ / _____ / _____

SPEECH & COMMUNICATION :

SOCIAL SKILLS :

SENSORY :

VESTIBULAR :

VISUAL :

TACTILE :

ORAL MOTOR :

AUDITORY :

FINE MOTOR :

THIS WEEK'S CHALLENGES :

THIS WEEK'S HIGHLIGHTS :

FAVORITE MOMENT :

Week 17 | Appointment

MON: ☐

TUE: ☐

WED: ☐

THU: ☐

FRI: ☐

SAT: ☐

SUN: ☐

Week **18** | **Child Goals**

Date : _____/_____/_____

_____ ☐
_____ ☐
_____ ☐
_____ ☐
_____ ☐
_____ ☐

SOCIAL SKILLS

_____ ☐
_____ ☐
_____ ☐
_____ ☐
_____ ☐
_____ ☐

SENSORY

_____ ☐
_____ ☐
_____ ☐
_____ ☐
_____ ☐
_____ ☐

Week 18 | Activities Days & Activity Ideas

MONDAY

TUESDAY

WEDNESDAY

THURSDAY

FRIDAY

SATURDAY

SUNDAY

FINE MOTOR ACTIVITIES

VESTIBULAR-PROPRIOCEPTIVE

TACTILE

VISUAL

ORAL

AUDITORY

NOTE

Week **18** | Goals & Progress **Tracker**

Date : _____ / _____ / _____

SPEECH & COMMUNICATION :

SOCIAL SKILLS :

SENSORY :

VESTIBULAR :

VISUAL :

TACTILE :

ORAL MOTOR :

AUDITORY :

FINE MOTOR :

THIS WEEK'S CHALLENGES :

THIS WEEK'S HIGHLIGHTS :

FAVORITE MOMENT :

☐

MON:

☐

TUE:

☐

WED:

☐

THU:

☐

FRI:

☐

SAT:

☐

SUN:

Week **19** | **Child Goals**

Date : ____/____/_____

SPEECH & COMMUNICATION

☐
☐
☐
☐
☐
☐

SOCIAL SKILLS

☐
☐
☐
☐
☐
☐

SENSORY

☐
☐
☐
☐
☐
☐

Week 19 | Activities Days & Activity Ideas

MONDAY

TUESDAY

WEDNESDAY

THURSDAY

FRIDAY

SATURDAY

SUNDAY

FINE MOTOR ACTIVITIES

VESTIBULAR-PROPRIOCEPTIVE

TACTILE

VISUAL

ORAL

AUDITORY

NOTE

Week 19

Goals & Progress
Tracker

Date : _____ / _____ / _____

SPEECH & COMMUNICATION :

SOCIAL SKILLS :

SENSORY :

VESTIBULAR :

VISUAL :

TACTILE :

ORAL MOTOR :

AUDITORY :

FINE MOTOR :

THIS WEEK'S CHALLENGES :

THIS WEEK'S HIGHLIGHTS :

FAVORITE MOMENT :

MON: ☐

TUE: ☐

WED: ☐

THU: ☐

FRI: ☐

SAT: ☐

SUN: ☐

NOTE

Week 20 | Child Goals

Date : _____ / _____ / _____

SPEECH & COMMUNICATION

_____ ☐
_____ ☐
_____ ☐
_____ ☐
_____ ☐
_____ ☐

SOCIAL SKILLS

_____ ☐
_____ ☐
_____ ☐
_____ ☐
_____ ☐
_____ ☐

SENSORY

_____ ☐
_____ ☐
_____ ☐
_____ ☐
_____ ☐
_____ ☐

Week 20 | Activities Days & Activity Ideas

MONDAY

TUESDAY

WEDNESDAY

THURSDAY

FRIDAY

SATURDAY

SUNDAY

FINE MOTOR ACTIVITIES

VESTIBULAR-PROPRIOCEPTIVE

TACTILE

VISUAL

ORAL

AUDITORY

NOTE

Week 20 | Goals & Progress Tracker

Date : _____/_____/_____

SPEECH & COMMUNICATION :

SOCIAL SKILLS :

SENSORY :

VESTIBULAR :

VISUAL :

TACTILE :

ORAL MOTOR :

AUDITORY :

FINE MOTOR :

THIS WEEK'S CHALLENGES :

THIS WEEK'S HIGHLIGHTS :

FAVORITE MOMENT :

Week 20 | Appointment

MON: ☐

TUE: ☐

WED: ☐

THU: ☐

FRI: ☐

SAT: ☐

SUN: ☐

Week **21** | **Child Goals**

Date : _____/_____/_____

☐
☐
☐
☐
☐
☐

☐
☐
☐
☐
☐
☐

☐
☐
☐
☐
☐
☐

Week 21 | Activities Days & Activity Ideas

MONDAY

TUESDAY

WEDNESDAY

THURSDAY

FRIDAY

SATURDAY

SUNDAY

FINE MOTOR ACTIVITIES

VESTIBULAR-PROPRIOCEPTIVE

TACTILE

VISUAL

ORAL

AUDITORY

NOTE

Week 21 | Goals & Progress
Tracker

Date : _____/_____/_____

SPEECH & COMMUNICATION :

SOCIAL SKILLS :

SENSORY :

VESTIBULAR :

VISUAL :

TACTILE :

ORAL MOTOR :

AUDITORY :

FINE MOTOR :

THIS WEEK'S CHALLENGES :

THIS WEEK'S HIGHLIGHTS :

FAVORITE MOMENT :

Week **21** | **Appointment**

MON: ☐

TUE: ☐

WED: ☐

THU: ☐

FRI: ☐

SAT: ☐

SUN: ☐

Week 22 | Child Goals

Date : _____/_____/_____

SPEECH & COMMUNICATION

_____ ☐
_____ ☐
_____ ☐
_____ ☐
_____ ☐
_____ ☐

SOCIAL SKILLS

_____ ☐
_____ ☐
_____ ☐
_____ ☐
_____ ☐
_____ ☐

SENSORY

_____ ☐
_____ ☐
_____ ☐
_____ ☐
_____ ☐
_____ ☐

Week 22 | Activities Days & Activity Ideas

MONDAY

TUESDAY

WEDNESDAY

THURSDAY

FRIDAY

SATURDAY

SUNDAY

FINE MOTOR ACTIVITIES

VESTIBULAR-PROPRIOCEPTIVE

TACTILE

VISUAL

ORAL

AUDITORY

NOTE

Week 22 | Goals & Progress Tracker

Date : _____ / _____ / _____

SPEECH & COMMUNICATION :

SOCIAL SKILLS :

SENSORY :

VESTIBULAR :

VISUAL :

TACTILE :

ORAL MOTOR :

AUDITORY :

FINE MOTOR :

THIS WEEK'S CHALLENGES :

THIS WEEK'S HIGHLIGHTS :

FAVORITE MOMENT :

Week 22 | Appointment

☐

MON:

☐

TUE:

☐

WED:

☐

THU:

☐

FRI:

☐

SAT:

☐

SUN:

Week 23 | Child Goals

Date : _____/_____/_____

SPEECH & COMMUNICATION

- [ ]
- [ ]
- [ ]
- [ ]
- [ ]
- [ ]

SOCIAL SKILLS

- [ ]
- [ ]
- [ ]
- [ ]
- [ ]
- [ ]

SENSORY

- [ ]
- [ ]
- [ ]
- [ ]
- [ ]
- [ ]

Week 23 | Activities Days & Activity Ideas

MONDAY

TUESDAY

WEDNESDAY

THURSDAY

FRIDAY

SATURDAY

SUNDAY

FINE MOTOR ACTIVITIES

VESTIBULAR-PROPRIOCEPTIVE

TACTILE

VISUAL

ORAL

AUDITORY

NOTE

Week 23 | Goals & Progress Tracker

Date : _____/_____/_____

SPEECH & COMMUNICATION :

SOCIAL SKILLS :

SENSORY :

VESTIBULAR :

VISUAL :

TACTILE :

ORAL MOTOR :

AUDITORY :

FINE MOTOR :

THIS WEEK'S CHALLENGES :

THIS WEEK'S HIGHLIGHTS :

FAVORITE MOMENT :

Week **23** | **Appointment**

MON: ☐

TUE: ☐

WED: ☐

THU: ☐

FRI: ☐

SAT: ☐

SUN: ☐

Week 24 | Child Goals

Date : _____/_____/_____

SPEECH & COMMUNICATION

_____ ☐
_____ ☐
_____ ☐
_____ ☐
_____ ☐
_____ ☐

SOCIAL SKILLS

_____ ☐
_____ ☐
_____ ☐
_____ ☐
_____ ☐
_____ ☐

SENSORY

_____ ☐
_____ ☐
_____ ☐
_____ ☐
_____ ☐
_____ ☐

Week 24 | Activities Days & Activity Ideas

MONDAY

TUESDAY

WEDNESDAY

THURSDAY

FRIDAY

SATURDAY

SUNDAY

FINE MOTOR ACTIVITIES

VESTIBULAR-PROPRIOCEPTIVE

TACTILE

VISUAL

ORAL

AUDITORY

NOTE

Week 24 | Goals & Progress
Tracker

Date : _____/_____/_____

SPEECH & COMMUNICATION :

SOCIAL SKILLS :

SENSORY :

VESTIBULAR :

VISUAL :

TACTILE :

ORAL MOTOR :

AUDITORY :

FINE MOTOR :

THIS WEEK'S CHALLENGES :

THIS WEEK'S HIGHLIGHTS :

FAVORITE MOMENT :

Week 24 | Appointment

MON: ☐

TUE: ☐

WED: ☐

THU: ☐

FRI: ☐

SAT: ☐

SUN: ☐

Week 25 | Child Goals

Date : _____/_____/_____

SPEECH & COMMUNICATION

☐
☐
☐
☐
☐
☐

SOCIAL SKILLS

☐
☐
☐
☐
☐
☐

SENSORY

☐
☐
☐
☐
☐
☐

Week 25 | Activities Days & Activity Ideas

MONDAY

TUESDAY

WEDNESDAY

THURSDAY

FRIDAY

SATURDAY

SUNDAY

FINE MOTOR ACTIVITIES

VESTIBULAR-PROPRIOCEPTIVE

TACTILE

VISUAL

ORAL

AUDITORY

NOTE

Week 25 | Goals & Progress **Tracker**

Date : _____/_____/_____

SPEECH & COMMUNICATION :

SOCIAL SKILLS :

SENSORY :

VESTIBULAR :

VISUAL :

TACTILE :

ORAL MOTOR :

AUDITORY :

FINE MOTOR :

THIS WEEK'S CHALLENGES :

THIS WEEK'S HIGHLIGHTS :

FAVORITE MOMENT :

Week 25 | Appointment

MON: ☐

TUE: ☐

WED: ☐

THU: ☐

FRI: ☐

SAT: ☐

SUN: ☐

NOTE

Week 26 | Child Goals

Date : _____ / _____ / _____

SPEECH & COMMUNICATION

_____ ☐
_____ ☐
_____ ☐
_____ ☐
_____ ☐
_____ ☐

SOCIAL SKILLS

_____ ☐
_____ ☐
_____ ☐
_____ ☐
_____ ☐
_____ ☐

SENSORY

_____ ☐
_____ ☐
_____ ☐
_____ ☐
_____ ☐
_____ ☐

Week 26 | Activities Days & Activity Ideas

MONDAY

TUESDAY

WEDNESDAY

THURSDAY

FRIDAY

SATURDAY

SUNDAY

FINE MOTOR ACTIVITIES

VESTIBULAR-PROPRIOCEPTIVE

TACTILE

VISUAL

ORAL

AUDITORY

NOTE

Week **26** | Goals & Progress **Tracker**

Date : _____/_____/_____

SPEECH & COMMUNICATION :

SOCIAL SKILLS :

SENSORY :

VESTIBULAR :

VISUAL :

TACTILE :

ORAL MOTOR :

AUDITORY :

FINE MOTOR :

THIS WEEK'S CHALLENGES :

THIS WEEK'S HIGHLIGHTS :

FAVORITE MOMENT :

Week 26 | Appointment

MON:

□

TUE:

□

WED:

□

THU:

□

FRI:

□

SAT:

□

SUN:

□

Week 27 | Child Goals

Date : _____/_____/_____

SPEECH & COMMUNICATION

- ☐
- ☐
- ☐
- ☐
- ☐
- ☐

SOCIAL SKILLS

- ☐
- ☐
- ☐
- ☐
- ☐
- ☐

SENSORY

- ☐
- ☐
- ☐
- ☐
- ☐
- ☐

Week 27 | Activities Days & Activity Ideas

MONDAY

TUESDAY

WEDNESDAY

THURSDAY

FRIDAY

SATURDAY

SUNDAY

FINE MOTOR ACTIVITIES

VESTIBULAR-PROPRIOCEPTIVE

TACTILE

VISUAL

ORAL

AUDITORY

NOTE

Week 27

Goals & Progress
Tracker

Date : _____/_____/_____

SPEECH & COMMUNICATION :

SOCIAL SKILLS :

SENSORY :

VESTIBULAR :

VISUAL :

TACTILE :

ORAL MOTOR :

AUDITORY :

FINE MOTOR :

THIS WEEK'S CHALLENGES :

THIS WEEK'S HIGHLIGHTS :

FAVORITE MOMENT :

Week **27** | **Appointment**

MON: ☐

TUE: ☐

WED: ☐

THU: ☐

FRI: ☐

SAT: ☐

SUN: ☐

NOTE

Week 28 | Child Goals

Date : _____/_____/_____

SPEECH & COMMUNICATION

_____ ☐
_____ ☐
_____ ☐
_____ ☐
_____ ☐
_____ ☐

SOCIAL SKILLS

_____ ☐
_____ ☐
_____ ☐
_____ ☐
_____ ☐
_____ ☐

SENSORY

_____ ☐
_____ ☐
_____ ☐
_____ ☐
_____ ☐
_____ ☐

Week 28 | Activities Days & Activity Ideas

MONDAY

TUESDAY

WEDNESDAY

THURSDAY

FRIDAY

SATURDAY

SUNDAY

FINE MOTOR ACTIVITIES

VESTIBULAR-PROPRIOCEPTIVE

TACTILE

VISUAL

ORAL

AUDITORY

NOTE

Week 28 | Goals & Progress
Tracker

Date : _____/_____/_____

SPEECH & COMMUNICATION :

SOCIAL SKILLS :

SENSORY :

VESTIBULAR :

VISUAL :

TACTILE :

ORAL MOTOR :

AUDITORY :

FINE MOTOR :

THIS WEEK'S CHALLENGES :

THIS WEEK'S HIGHLIGHTS :

FAVORITE MOMENT :

Week **28** | **Appointment**

MON: ☐

TUE: ☐

WED: ☐

THU: ☐

FRI: ☐

SAT: ☐

SUN: ☐

Week 29 | Child Goals

Date : _____/_____/_____

SPEECH & COMMUNICATION

_____ ☐
_____ ☐
_____ ☐
_____ ☐
_____ ☐
_____ ☐

SOCIAL SKILLS

_____ ☐
_____ ☐
_____ ☐
_____ ☐
_____ ☐
_____ ☐

SENSORY

_____ ☐
_____ ☐
_____ ☐
_____ ☐
_____ ☐
☐

Week 29 | Activities Days & Activity Ideas

MONDAY

TUESDAY

WEDNESDAY

THURSDAY

FRIDAY

SATURDAY

SUNDAY

FINE MOTOR ACTIVITIES

VESTIBULAR-PROPRIOCEPTIVE

TACTILE

VISUAL

ORAL

AUDITORY

NOTE

Week 29 | Goals & Progress
Tracker

Date : _____/_____/_____

SPEECH & COMMUNICATION :

SOCIAL SKILLS :

SENSORY :

VESTIBULAR :

VISUAL :

TACTILE :

ORAL MOTOR :

AUDITORY :

FINE MOTOR :

THIS WEEK'S CHALLENGES :

THIS WEEK'S HIGHLIGHTS :

FAVORITE MOMENT :

Week 29 | Appointment

MON:

☐

TUE:

☐

WED:

☐

THU:

☐

FRI:

☐

SAT:

☐

SUN:

☐

www.ingramcontent.com/pod-product-compliance
Lightning Source LLC
Chambersburg PA
CBHW080252030426
42334CB00023BA/2790